THE DELIGHTFUL, DELICIOUS DAYLILY

Recipes and More

Second Edition

by

Peter A. Gail, Ph.D.

Foreword by
Cathy Wilkinson Barash

Goosefoot Acres Press
CLEVELAND, OHIO

Cover and Illustrations by Robert Tubbesing

Printed in the United States of America

ISBN 1-879863-60-X

Published by:

Goosefoot Acres Press
Division of Goosefoot Acres, Inc.
P.O. Box 18016
Cleveland, OH 44118-0016
(216) 932-2145

9 7 5 3 2 4 6 8

About The Author

Dr. Peter A. Gail, Director of Goosefoot Acres Center for Wild Vegetable Research and Education, earned degrees in biology and botany from California State Polytechnic University and Claremont Graduate School and his Ph.D. in botany from Rutgers University. Until 1988 he was Associate Professor of Urban and Environmental Studies at Cleveland State University, where he lectured and wrote about food and medicinal uses of backyard weeds. Wild vegetable foraging was part of his courses.

Gail has researched recipes and folklore about ethnic uses of wild plants for more than 30 years, and has authored numerous articles and several books on the subject, including *The Dandelion Celebration: A Guide to Unexpected Cuisine*. His column on the uses of backyard weeds, "On The Trail Of The Volunteer Vegetable," appears regularly in local newspapers and in *The Business of Herbs*, a trade journal for herb growers and marketers. Dr. Gail also shares his research and experiences in workshops and lectures on edible wild plants throughout the United States.

Acknowledgments

Thanks go to Ray Hallenstein, my next-door neighbor who inspired this work in the first place, to Judi Strauss for clarifying recipes and various points in the text, to Lee and Diana Bristol and Angelo Cerchione for their valuable suggestions, to Cathy Wilkinson Barash for her technical and editorial advice and for writing the Foreword, to Bob Tubbesing for the illustrations and his continuing artistic advice, and to Ann Marie Stockmaster and Rebecca Chandler for their editorial assistance.

I also thank my loving wife, Wilma, for helping to test and refine recipes and certain sections of the text, and for her faithful support and encouragement over the years. I'm sure few other men are greeted with such patient understanding and cooperation when they mention ideas to their spouses about eating the flower garden!

As this is a compilation of recipes from a variety of sources, none of which are original, I also thank those who developed and published these recipes in the first place. Credits appear with the recipes, and full references to the works are found in Chapter 7.

Foreword

To my mind, "delightful" and "delicious" are the two best adjectives to describe daylilies, as well as this book. Sitting in my basement office in the cold of winter, reading the manuscript, my mind takes flight, and my mouth begins to water as I look at each recipe. I can almost taste Mandarin Pancakes with Mu Shu Vegetables. As I own the *Sundays at Moosewood* cookbook, I wonder how I could have missed these mouth-watering recipes.

That is the essence of this book. Peter Gail admits that he has not come up with anything new on the daylily front. What he has done that is so wonderful is to pore through the classic cookbooks as well as some more esoteric ones and distill the information into one concise volume. I would expect a book such as *The Chinese Restaurant Cookbook* or *Madame Wu's Art of Chinese Cooking* to have daylily recipes, having learned, while researching my own book, that Chinese hot and sour soup is somewhat like Jewish chicken soup. Every cook has a variation, but certain ingredients can be found in all recipes. In the case of Chinese hot and sour soup, dried daylilies (golden needles) are one of the staples. What surprised me, in perusing this book, was that *The Joy of Cooking* has daylily recipes. I am now inspired to browse through my cookbooks, one by one, and see what other gems are hidden on their pages.

The range of complexity of the recipes makes this book appealing even to gardeners who don't fancy themselves as cooks, and to great cooks who don't fancy themselves as gardeners, but who may have a stand of old-fashioned daylilies in the corner of their property. From my simple recipe for sautéed daylilies that calls for only three ingredients to the more complex aspic-filled daylily blossoms (which seems to demand more manual dexterity than fine cooking skills), to the time-consuming Mu Shu vegetables, there are recipes in this book to fit any level of cooking skill or time available to cook.

This book combines a healthy dose of caution, lore, scientific fact and appetizing recipes to make it a classic in its field. My only regret is that, as I write this, it is mid-winter, and I cannot run out to my garden and start trying some of these recipes myself. The snow and ice prevent me even from digging up some daylily tubers. I can't wait for the first daylily shoots of spring!!

Cathy Wilkinson Barash
Author of *Edible Flowers: From Garden to Palate*
(Fulcrum Press)
17 February 1995

Preface

Ever since we moved to Cleveland Heights, Ohio in the 1970's, our driveway has been bordered with beautiful, bright orange daylily blossoms (*Hemerocallis fulva*). We didn't plant them, and we have done nothing to encourage them. In fact, we take them for granted. All the same, they grow on. No diseases affect them; no insects carve holes in their leaves and the fragrant blossoms open their cheery faces to grace our yard every year in the early summer.

We recently bought property in Ashtabula County, Ohio. Who was there to greet us? You guessed it. Our quiet, uncomplaining, ever-present friend, the daylily!

Daylilies are so easy to take for granted that we fail to realize what an incredible resource they are. Not only do they give beauty and fragrance year after year, they also provide an excellent year-round food supply. In fall, winter, and early spring, when we want something exotic, we harvest and serve the small, white "tubers"[1] attached

---

[1] "Tuber" refers to the swollen root ends of the daylily. They are not true tubers, which are fleshy swellings of underground stems (rhizomes) and contain buds from which new shoots arise.

to the ends of daylily roots, which are crisp like water chestnuts. During the summer growing season, buds, flowers, and young pods can be included in soups, fritters, and breads, as well as such dishes as **Sausage Tarts, Chicken Daylily Commotion, Confetti Biscuits, Chicken Salad Special,** and many others which fill the pages of this book.

This little book was initially inspired by our neighbors who felt somewhat overwhelmed by the wealth of daylilies which bordered their yard and ours. When they asked, "What good are they?" I couldn't resist telling them. And, because one ought not keep a good thing to oneself, I decided to share the information and recipes with you also. Nutritious and tasty vegetables which grow innocently in our gardens disguised as flowers are worth knowing about. The recipes included here will let you add the exotic and elegant flavor of daylilies to your meals and give your wallet a break at the same time. For, as you will discover, daylilies are much more than just pretty faces!

Daylilies, in addition to being important in Oriental cuisine, also have specific uses in Oriental medicine. Describing such uses, however, is beyond the scope of this book. I am not a medical doctor and neither advocate nor prescribe daylilies for any medical purpose. Some writers (see page 15) have made observations regarding possible side effects from using daylilies as food. They are included because I felt that you should have this information before you try daylilies for the first time.

If you know or suspect that you have specific illnesses, chronic conditions, or food-related or other allergies, contact your physician before trying daylilies and share this information with him/her. I assume no liability for omissions or for the use or misuse of the information contained in this book.

Please send comments, additions, and other suggestions to **Peter A. Gail, Ph.D., Goosefoot Acres Center for Wild Vegetable Research and Education, P.O. Box 18016, Cleveland Heights, OH 44118.**

Peter A. Gail, Ph.D.
May, 1995

Contents

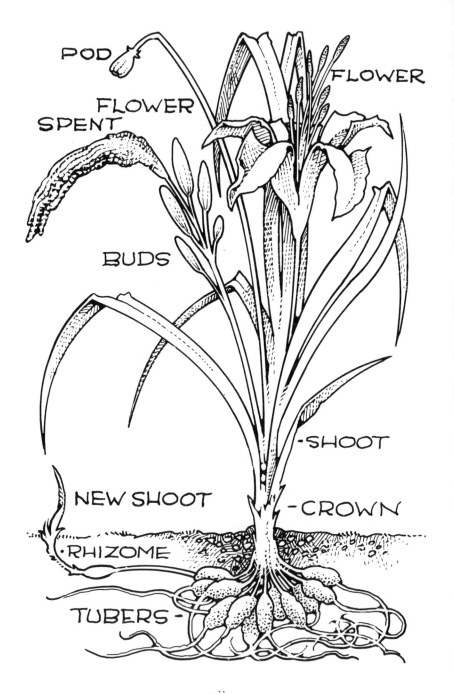

POD

FLOWER

SPENT FLOWER

FLOWER

BUDS

SHOOT

NEW SHOOT

CROWN

RHIZOME

TUBERS

Chapter 1

An Asian Affair

In China, daylily flowers and their unopened buds have been a respected and venerable part of regional cuisine since at least 304 A.D. when Chi Han wrote about them in *An Introduction to Daylily*. They are, in fact, major ingredients in such famous Asian dishes as Mu-Shu Pork and Hot and Sour Soup, and are widely eaten throughout Asia today.

Dr. Darrel Apps, one of the most prominent daylily breeders in the United States, reports that he encountered a wide variety of food products made from daylilies, including sugared daylily flowers, in the Lotte Shopping Center in Seoul, Korea. He also found that daylilies were so popular as food with the locals on a small island off the Korean coast that not a flower was to be found anywhere except right along the coastal strand. When he asked why those on the shoreline were spared, he was told that the beach was still covered with land mines from the war and it was too dangerous to collect there. The islanders told him that they dig up the shoots and eat them like asparagus in spring, and then eat the buds and flowers later in the season.

The wild species of daylily are native to China, Japan, and Korea. They so captured the imagination of flower fanciers that tens of thousands of cultivars (hybrids) have been produced over the past 100 years, beginning with the work of George Yeld, an English schoolteacher, in 1890. These have joined their wild relatives here in America.

You can buy an eight ounce bag of dried daylily flower buds in any Asian grocery store in the United States under the names "dried lily buds", "golden needles" or "gum jum." Or, you can harvest these same flower buds for free in your garden!

The flavor of daylily buds and flowers varies with the variety. The fresh buds have been compared in taste to something between green beans and asparagus. Since flavor is strongly influenced by scent, the more fragrant daylily cultivars may taste sweeter than those without a strong scent. According to *Madame Wu's Art of Chinese Cooking* (Wu 1973), dried daylily buds have a mild beef broth flavor. Dr. Apps reports that the phytocyanin pigments, which create red flowers, are bitter, while the carotenoid pigments found in yellow flowers are not. Pigmentation all begins with the red/yellow mix in the orange wild type *H. fulva* and is bred from there toward either yellow or red, with many variegates in between. Given this, if color were the only factor determining flavor, the yellow flowers should be the most tasty.

Because daylilies have long been a significant part of Asian cuisine, several Oriental recipes are included in this book which call for ingredients other than daylilies that may not be carried in your local grocery store. If you do not recognize an ingredient required by a particular recipe, check with your local Asian market or specialty store for that ingredient or an appropriate substitute.

While most parts of the daylily are edible, you should be aware that:

- Delena Tull[2] warns that daylilies can create a mild laxative effect, and if eaten raw, the green buds may cause throat irritation. She also warns that the leaves of narcissus, iris, and daffodils, which are poisonous, somewhat resemble daylily leaves, so you must make sure you know what you are gathering.

- In a letter to **The Wild Food Forum** (December 1991), Ellen Elliot Weatherbee, author of *Edible Wild Plants: A Guide to Collecting and Cooking*, writes that students in her foraging classes at the University of Michigan have experienced upset stomachs, and, in one case, swollen testicles, from eating daylilies. She says that tubers, buds, and flowers have all caused problems. Chemical research on daylily plant parts reveals nothing which could cause such problems. She does note, however, that many of the plants eaten were collected from along roadsides, and could have been contaminated by automobile pollutants and/or herbicides. Sid Berman of the Wildthymers, a foraging group in Virginia, reports similar problems in the Shenandoah Valley.

---

[2]   *A Practical Guide to Edible and Useful Plants,* Texas Monthly Press, Austin, Texas.

- According to Foster and Chongxi (1991) the young shoots of the orange daylily, *Hemerocallis fulva,* may be potentially hallucinogenic in large doses.

- Dr. James Duke (1992), while reporting that he enjoys ten to twenty buds a day which he forages for lunch and eats raw, says that the tubers give him diarrhea, whether eaten raw or cooked.

- The daylily root is highly toxic and, while valued in Asian folk medicine, should never be used except under medical supervision.

Cooked daylily buds and flowers have caused me diarrhea and stomach cramps when eaten in large quantities. To avoid those problems, I now eat them sparingly for the first two or three days of the season until my digestive system gets used to them, and I always eat them in moderation. If you choose to use daylilies, I encourage you to do the same.

Because of these considerations, daylilies should always be used with caution until you discover your own reaction to them, and should **never** be used medicinally except under the direction of competent health professionals who thoroughly understand the characteristics of the plant.

As said in the Preface, if you know or suspect that you have specific illnesses, chronic conditions, or food-related or other allergies, contact your physician before trying daylilies.

The facts that the daylily is a hardy perennial, appears spring after spring with no work on our part, is unaffected by bugs and diseases, supplies a profusion of buds and flowers, has been a staple in Chinese cuisine for so many centuries, and because so many people eat it without adverse effect, make it, even with these cautions, a vegetable worth serious consideration.

Nutritious and tasty vegetables which grow innocently in our gardens disguised as flowers are worth knowing about.

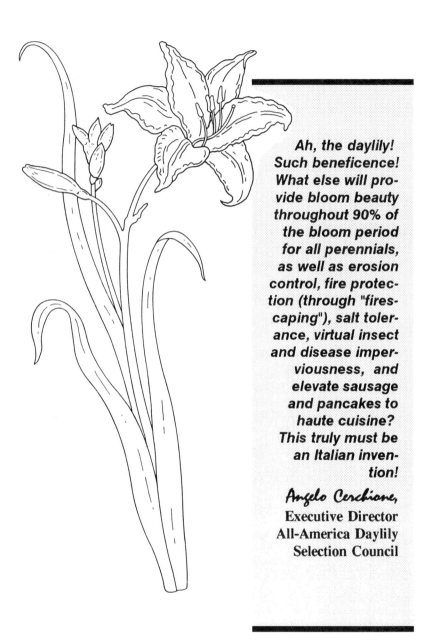

Ah, the daylily! Such beneficence! What else will provide bloom beauty throughout 90% of the bloom period for all perennials, as well as erosion control, fire protection (through "firescaping"), salt tolerance, virtual insect and disease imperviousness, and elevate sausage and pancakes to haute cuisine? This truly must be an Italian invention!

Angelo Cerchione,
**Executive Director
All-America Daylily
Selection Council**

Chapter 2

Selecting and Growing Daylilies

T he best information about how to start propagating daylilies is contained in *Daylilies: The Beginner's Handbook,* available from the American Hemerocallis Society, 1454 Rebel Drive, Jackson, Mississippi 39211-6334 [Tel: (601) 366-4362].

Lee Bristol, owner of Bloomingfields Farm in Gaylordsville, Connecticut, says that daylily cultivars are now available which bloom at different times throughout the growing season.

According to Bristol, daylilies can be planted any time throughout the year, but if planted in fall, they should be mulched. They are sun-loving flowers but bloom equally well in partial shade if they get at least six hours of sunshine per day. They do not grow well in either low, wet spots or high, dry spots over thin soil, but do like a lot of moisture just before and during the blooming season. A catalog of 100 daylily varieties and full instructions for the planting and care of daylilies can be had by writing Bloomingfields Farm, Box 5, Gaylordsville, Connecticut 06755-0005 [Tel: (203) 354-6951].

Other sources for daylilies may be found in *Eureka! Daylily Reference Guide, 1995,* by Ken Gregory, 5586 Quail Creek Drive, Granite Falls, NC 28630-9538 [Tel: (704)396-6107]. In its 225 pages are listings for some 80 nurseries and farms which grow daylilies either exclusively or as their major crop. According to Lee Bristol, "these are the 80 which paid to be listed. Some other well-known growers did not pay and are not listed." Bristol suspects that there "may be about 150 substantial sources of daylilies in the U.S., and many, many additional local sources which carry one or two dozen cultivars." The 1994 edition of *Eureka* listed 10,280 cultivars.

In addition, each spring, the American Hemerocallis Society's **Daylily Journal** includes a comprehensive directory of daylily sources and AHS Display Gardens throughout the United States.

You may also check the yellow pages and/or garden centers for daylily sources in your area.

Chapter 3

Recipes for Tubers and Shoots

From fall through early spring, daylily tubers are in their prime — filled with starches and sugars stored from the past summer and ready to be released into spring's new growth! Since wild-type daylilies are prolific dividers, taking a mess of tubers now and then from any reasonably large patch amounts to nothing more than thinning it. Make sure, however, that you leave enough tubers to start your crop next year! Don't do this with your expensive hybrids. Since they don't divide, you will eliminate them and end up with a mighty pricey supper.

Each roadside daylily plant has old roots, new roots, and rhizomes. From midspring through early summer, each plant produces as many as six rhizomes, each putting up a single shoot at its end. Young roots, which extend downward from these new shoots, produce swellings near their tips which resemble tubers. The young tubers are tender, white, filled with starch and sugars, and edible both raw and cooked. As they get older, they become firmer, and by fall they are hard, filled with the nutrients required to "jump start" the new growth in spring.

Root tissue leading into and out of these tubers is not edible, however. It contains colchicine, rhein and hemerocallin, all of which are poisonous when taken in large doses, and which seem to accumulate in the system. Chinese studies suggest that eating too much root at one time can cause blindness, respiratory problems and lack of bladder control. These studies also suggest that eating even small amounts of roots over many years might ultimately affect the eyesight and even cause blindness. As the roots mature, the concentration of these chemicals increases.

I have found no specific precautions in the literature about eating tubers. However, the tubers might, being a part of the root, also contain small quantities of these chemicals. Consequently, eat tubers sparingly until you discover your own tolerance for them.

Some plants have more tubers, others fewer. Lee Bristol told me that "age and soil have a marked effect on the number of swollen root ends on quite a few varieties. Wet soils, especially, encourage the development of swollen roots on some varieties which show very few on dry soils. Some varieties are 99% without swollen roots, but others (including the roadside daylily), have 100% of the roots swollen."

Some cultivars also produce an occasional rhizome which will give rise to several plants along its length. Each scale mark on these rhizomes contains a potential bud for the development of a new plant in addition to the dominant bud at the rhizome tip which always develops. However, most cultivars, some of which can cost hundreds of dollars per plant, **do not reproduce** this way. Therefore, do not eat tubers and shoots from these cultivars, because doing so will kill the plants.

In late fall and early spring, the white tubers are crisp like water chestnuts. They can be gathered, scrubbed thoroughly, and eaten raw in salads, cooked in Oriental dishes, boiled for 15 minutes and creamed or mashed and fried into fritters, baked like potatoes, or steamed and served as an appetizer with dip.

According to the American Hemerocallis Society, the young tubers have sometimes been used as an acceptable substitute for peas after the skin is scraped off with a fingernail. They remain cool and crisp like water chestnuts even after being cooked and can be added raw to salads or cooked in Chinese recipes.

The easiest way to try daylily tubers is to gather them, wash them, and pop them into your mouth or add them to a green salad. You don't need a recipe for that! If you want to get a bit fancier, you might want to try some of the following:

Daylily Tubers with Potatoes

Gather firm tubers in spring or fall. Wash and scrub, removing all roots and hairs. Add wild onions or leeks plus the daylily tubers to grated, boiled potatoes and fry in butter or oil until tender and browned.

Daylily Tubers in Chinese Stir Fry

Scrub tubers of daylilies and use in stir-fried dishes as you would use water chestnuts.

Wildman Steve Brill recommends cooking the swollen root ends like potatoes, cutting a hole in the skin and then squirting out the contents, like toothpaste out of a tube.
James Duke, *Handbook of Edible Weeds*

Daylily Stuffed Tomatoes

4 tomatoes
½ cup daylily tubers, peeled and diced
2 Tbs. chickweed or spinach (gathered from the garden), chopped
4 Tbs. chives or ½ tsp. finely chopped onion
2 hard-boiled eggs, diced
3 Tbs. mayonnaise

Prepare tomatoes by washing, removing stems, and quartering ⅔ of the way through, so the tomato opens like a four-pointed star. Mix other ingredients together and stuff in tomatoes. Serves 4.

(Russell 1975)

If you like something a bit spicier, here is a Mexican recipe, called:

Consuelo's Recipe

3 cups daylily tubers, cooked and peeled
1½ cups chicken stock
1 red pepper, chopped
1 strip bacon
2 oz. sharp cheddar cheese, grated

In a saucepan, combine daylily tubers, chicken stock, and red pepper. Cook until pepper is tender.

Dice and fry bacon, and add both bacon and fat to the mixture. Add cheese and stir until melted. Serves 4-6.

(Russell 1975)

And finally, try this on your guests at your next spring party.

Daylily Dippers

50 + daylily tubers, scrubbed well

Dip

¼ cup sour cream
⅛ cup mayonnaise
½ cup yogurt
1 cup cottage cheese
1 Tbs. good French mustard
1 Tbs. red wine vinegar
1 clove garlic, crushed
    chopped parsley and scallion
    salt and pepper to taste

Remove rootlets and scrub the tubers. Steam the tubers over medium heat until tender.

Combine remaining ingredients in a small mixing bowl. Stick a toothpick in each tuber. Place bowl in the middle of a plate and arrange the tubers around it.

Young shoots are often cooked as an early green or stir-fry vegetable. One Chinese name for *Hemerocallis fulva* is **Xaun Cao**, which means "forget worry herb." This supposedly refers to the reputed sedating effect that too large a dose of tender, young leaf shoots might have on you! If you decide to use the young shoots, be careful when harvesting to make sure they are not young shoots of daffodils, narcissus or iris, which somewhat resemble daylily shoots but are poisonous.

The white heart of the early spring shoots and the green shoots themselves before they open make an excellent vegetable, which, according to Gibbons (1966), is rich in Vitamins A and C. The young shoots can be steamed or boiled for 5-10 minutes, seasoned to taste with melted butter, salt, and pepper and eaten like asparagus. They can be tossed raw into salads, served on a plate with dip, or sautéed and added to cheese omelets.

If you miss the young spring greens, you have a second chance in late summer and early fall when new growth appears in among the spent leaves of summer, now a ghastly yellow and lying on the ground. These new, fresh greens grow straight up from the base, and can be harvested and chopped up for adding to salads and/or cooked greens.

Chapter 4

Recipes for Buds

Dried or fresh, unopened flower buds are used in both China and the U.S. primarily in soups and as a condiment and thickener in meat dishes. Chinese call these buds **Jin-zhen-cai**. They have a mucilaginous, somewhat sweet taste. Daylily flower buds are found in the kitchens of every good Chinese restaurant, and numerous North American edible plant guides mention cooked daylily buds as an delicacy.

Flowers and flower buds, because they are plentiful and disposable, can be used from both wild and hybrid plants. Buds vary in size, depending on the cultivar, from about ½ inch to 3 inches. For cooking, we normally gather them when they are between 1½ and 2 inches long. Lee Bristol prefers them at about 1¼ inches.

Daylily buds and blossoms have almost as much protein as spinach, more Vitamin A than string beans, and about the same amount of Vitamin C as orange juice.

Because the buds are so prolific, picking some for dinner a day or so before they open into full bloom has little effect on the floral display. They may also be harvested while in full bloom or after the blossoms are spent.

It is often the spent blossoms, picked the day after flowering, which are used to thicken soups, stews, and in the Mu-Shu Pork recipe below.

The best flavored buds are the most mature -- the ones which will turn into the next day's flowers. However, daylily buds have a tendency to open when dropped in hot water. If you want them to stay closed, pick them about two days before they are scheduled to open.

The buds and spent flowers may be frozen for use in the off-season. Blanch the buds in a kettle of water which has been brought to a rolling boil. Drop in only enough buds to be covered by the water. After the water returns to a boil, blanch for 3 minutes. Remove, chill in cold water, drain well and pack in freezer bags.

The flower buds and spent flowers may also be dehydrated by placing them on the racks of your dehydrator at 120°.

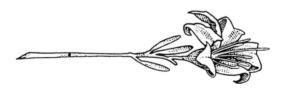

The most basic method of preparing daylily flower buds is to sauté them in butter, which is the way attendees at the 1991 American Hemerocallis Society Conference in Minneapolis enjoyed them.

Sautéed Daylily Buds

2 cups daylily buds
3 Tbs. butter
2 Tbs. chopped scallions
1 tsp. tarragon
1 tsp. dried parsley
½ tsp. salt
¼ tsp. pepper

Wash and drain the daylily buds. Dry and sauté in a skillet with butter and scallions for five minutes. Add the tarragon, parsley, salt and pepper. Sauté for another five minutes, stirring frequently. Serve hot. Makes an excellent vegetable side dish to go with most meats. Serves 4.

Billy Joe Tatum's Daylily Buds

2 cups daylily buds
4 Tbs. butter (½ stick)
¼ cup water
½ tsp. salt
    freshly ground black pepper to taste
¼ cup chopped leeks or wild onions (optional)

Rinse, drain, and pat the daylily buds dry. Melt butter in a skillet, add daylily buds, and sauté until tender. Add water and salt and simmer for 5 minutes. Wild onions or leeks can be added for additional flavor. Ms. Tatum says that they are "a delicious vegetable, with a flavor akin to green beans but milder." Serves 4.

(Tatum 1976)

Deep-Fried Daylily Buds

½ cup flour
1 egg, beaten
1 cup beer
1 tsp. salt
1 tsp. dried tarragon
2 egg whites, beaten stiff, until frothy
2 cups daylily buds
    Oil for deep frying

Beat together the flour, egg, beer, salt, and tarragon. Fold in the egg whites. Heat oil to sizzling. Dip the daylily buds in the batter. Fry until golden and puffy. Serves 4.

These deep-fried buds taste great served with the following quick and easy sauce which comes from *The Blue Strawbery Cookbook*:

Blue Strawbery Dipping Sauce

1 stick (½ cup) butter or margarine
2-3 minced shallots
⅛ tsp. saffron
    salt and pepper to taste

Melt butter. Add remaining ingredients and pour over fried daylily buds.

(Haller 1976)

According to **Madame Wu's Art of Chinese Cooking**, *the dried buds have a mild beef broth flavor, making daylily buds ideal as a source of a beef-flavored vegetarian soup stock.*

Daylily Buds Oriental Style

3 cups daylily buds, rinsed, drained and patted dry
  with paper towels
1 cup water
1 Tbs. mild vinegar
¼ cup chopped pecans or almonds
1 Tbs. soy sauce, preferably imported
  salt to taste
  hot cooked rice to serve 6.

Combine daylily buds and water in a saucepan and bring to
a boil. Simmer gently 15 minutes, or until buds are tender.
Drain off most of the cooking water, leaving only a
tablespoon or two. Add vinegar, nuts, soy sauce. Season
to taste. Stir well and serve hot over rice. Serves 6.

(Tatum 1976)

Daylily Buds Almandine

2 cups green daylily buds
2 Tbs. butter
1 cup sliced canned mushrooms, drained
½ cup slivered almonds
1 tsp. soy sauce

Pick 2 cups of green, unopened flower buds of daylilies
that seem ready to bloom in about two days. Cover the
cleaned daylily buds with salted water. Cover and boil for
1 minute. Pour off the water and drain. Heat the butter in
a skillet and sauté the daylily buds quickly with the canned
mushrooms. Add the almonds and soy sauce and toss
lightly. Serve at once. Serves 4.

(Kluger 1984)

Daylily buds are also excellent in minestrone soup, if you have the time and patience to make it.

Daylily Bud Minestrone Soup

2 cups dry white beans
  water
3 cups daylily buds
1 cup green beans, cut in 1" pieces
1 cup potatoes, diced
1 cup scallions or green onions, chopped
1 tsp. salt
1 clove garlic, crushed
2 Tbs. fresh basil, chopped
6 Tbs. tomato paste or home-canned tomato sauce
½ cup Parmesan cheese, grated
½ cup olive oil
½ cup spaghetti, broken
⅓ cup bread crumbs
  salt and pepper to taste
  pinch of saffron

Place the beans in a saucepan with water to cover and soak overnight. Drain. Cover with fresh water and simmer for 1½ hours. In a large kettle, bring 3 quarts of water to a boil. Add the daylilies, green beans, potatoes, scallions or green onions and salt. Simmer for 20 minutes.

While this is simmering, beat together the garlic, basil, tomato paste, Parmesan cheese, and olive oil. Blend together well. Drain the white beans and add to the soup. Add the broken spaghetti, bread crumbs, salt, pepper, and saffron. Simmer for 20 minutes.

Just before serving, beat the tomato, cheese, and basil mixture into the soup. Serve hot with warmed French or Italian bread. This soup is really delicious and is a meal in itself, and the use of so many vegetables other than the daylily makes this a true minestrone.

(Crowhurst n.d.)

Daylily buds can also be pickled so that they may be enjoyed out of season. They make a tasty and unusual addition to holiday relish trays.

Pickled Daylily Buds

1 cup cider vinegar
½ cup water
1 clove garlic, crushed
1 tsp. mustard seed
1 tsp. dill seed
½ tsp. non-iodized salt
¼ tsp. pepper
4 cups daylily buds

Boil the vinegar, water, garlic, mustard seed, dill seed, salt, and pepper for 10 minutes. While that mixture is cooking, place the daylily buds in a saucepan, cover with water and boil for 3 minutes. Drain well and pack into one quart or two one-pint sterilized canning jar(s). Pour vinegar mixture over the daylily buds. Seal tightly and refrigerate. Let sit for three weeks before using. Makes one quart.

(Crowhurst n.d.)

Daylily Tempura

1 can beer
1 cup all-purpose flour
4 cups daylily buds, 1¼" long
  salt
  flour for dusting
2 cups oil

Beat beer and flour together until frothy, then allow to sit for three hours. Dust the washed and drained daylily buds with flour, then dip into the batter and deep fry in oil (about 375°F) until golden brown. Serve with an avocado dip made as follows:

2 ripe avocados
¼ cup mayonnaise
1 garlic clove, crushed
2 Tbs. lemon juice
  dash of tabasco

Peel and mash the avocados and combine with the remaining ingredients. Chill at least one hour before serving. Fried daylilies make an interesting hors d'oeuvre.

(Smith 1973)

The flower buds are the most delicious part of this plant. All sizes of buds may be eaten, although I prefer the smallest ones, picked before the color shows. They may be cooked in any manner in which green beans are fixed, or they may be pickled, sautéed, or fried in fritters.
Billy Joe Tatum, *Wild Foods Cookbook*

Another delightful recipe from Crowhurst combines both daylily buds and opened daylily blossoms.

Chinese Daylilies

    1 cup celery, lettuce, or the white part of cabbage, washed and cut into 2 inch strips
    ½ cup mushrooms, sliced
    ¾ cup fresh or frozen green peas
    ⅓ cup scallions or onions, chopped
    ½ cup bean sprouts
    ½ cup bamboo shoots
    6 water chestnuts or daylily tubers
    3 Tbs. oil
    2 cups daylily buds
    1 cup chicken or vegetable stock
    1 Tbs. cornstarch (optional)
      soy sauce
    4 opened daylily blossoms

In a large bowl, combine all the vegetables above. In a large, heavy skillet or wok, heat the oil and sauté the vegetables and daylily buds until tender. Add the stock and simmer for 2 minutes. Add soy sauce to taste. For a slightly thicker sauce, dissolve cornstarch in a little of the chicken broth before adding to the vegetable mixture.

Place on a platter and garnish with the reserved daylily blossoms. Serve hot on its own or with cooked chicken or shrimp. Makes 4 servings.

(Crowhurst n.d.)

If you want to get really fancy, try these classic recipes. They are much simpler to make than it would seem from the mystique surrounding them in Asian restaurants.

Mu Shu Pork

  2 Tbs. dried tree ear mushrooms
10 dried daylily buds
  ¼ lb. boneless pork or 2 pork chops (½-inch thick), trimmed, boned and cut into ⅛-inch square strips, about 2 inches long (equal to 1/2 cup of strips)
  3 oz. bamboo shoots
  1 scallion
2½ Tbs. peanut or corn oil
  1 tsp. sesame oil
Mandarin Pancakes (see recipe on page 38)

Soak tree ear mushrooms and daylily buds separately in a generous amount of warm water for at least 20 minutes or until softened. Rinse tree ears well. Cut off any hard wood, then cut the large pieces into 2 or 3 smaller pieces. Pinch off hard ends of daylily buds; cut in half. Set the tree ears and lily buds on a plate. Shred 3 oz. bamboo shoots in strips ⅛ inch square by 2 inches long. Combine on the plate with tree ears and lily buds. Cut scallion, including the tender green parts, into 2-inch pieces, smash with the side of a cleaver and cut in long shreds. Set aside separately from other ingredients.

Egg Curds

3 eggs
¼ tsp. salt

Beat eggs with salt in a small bowl just enough to blend yolks and whites. Cover if not using immediately.

Seasoning Sauce

    1 Tbs. light soy sauce
    1 tsp. rice wine or dry sherry
    1 tsp. sugar

Combine ingredients in a cup.

    Heat a wok over medium-low heat. When hot, swirl in 1½ Tbs. of peanut oil to coat bottom and part way up the sides. Add the eggs; lift and stir slowly to scramble until soft curds form. They should be golden yellow and moist, not dry and brown. Remove to a plate.

    If any traces of egg remain in the wok, rinse, then reheat over highest heat. Add the remaining 1 Tbs. oil. When hot, add pork and stir-fry until shreds turn color and separate (less than 1 minute.) Add the Seasoning Sauce; mix well. Add tree ear mushrooms, daylily buds, and bamboo shoots. Stir-fry 1 minute longer.

    Return the egg curds to the wok. Add the shredded scallion; stir to mix well and reheat the egg curds, breaking them up if necessary.

    Remove contents of wok to a serving bowl. Splash on the 1 tsp. sesame oil. Serve hot with steamed Mandarin pancakes.

                           (Myers 1984)

    Traditionally, tortilla-like pancakes are served with Mu Shu dishes. If you're feeling pressed for time and/or are feeling lazy, flour tortillas from the market make an acceptable, though not nearly as good, substitute. Steam them for 3 or 4 minutes before using.

Mandarin Pancakes

2 cups unbleached white flour
¾ cup boiling water
1 Tbs. dark sesame oil

Mound the flour in a mixing bowl. Gradually add boiling water while mixing with a spoon to form a smooth dough. Knead the dough in a bowl for 4 to 5 minutes. Form it into a ball, cover it with a towel, and let it rest for 20 minutes.

Knead the dough on a lightly floured surface for a couple of minutes. Shape it into a long cylinder, 1½ inches in diameter by about 14 inches long. Cut this cylinder into twelve equal pieces, each a little more than an inch wide. Flatten each piece between the palms of your hands to form a round 2 ½" in diameter. Lightly brush one side of each slice with sesame oil and then place the oiled side of a second slice against it. In other words, you will have six pairs, oiled face to oiled face. Using a rolling pin, gently roll out each pancake pair to an 8-inch round. Thinness is important or the pancake will be chewy.

Heat a cast-iron skillet on medium heat for 2 to 3 minutes. Cook each pancake pair in the unoiled pan for a couple of minutes on each side or until just speckled brown. Place on a plate to cool for a few seconds before peeling the pancakes apart. Separate the pancakes and stack on a plate covered with a damp cloth.

If you're preparing the Mandarin Pancakes in advance, you may cover and refrigerate them for one week or freeze them for up to three months. Reheat the pancakes in a steamer before serving.

(Moosewood Collective 1990)

Mu Shu Vegetables

¼ cup dried daylily buds (golden needles)
2 Tbs. dried tree ear mushrooms
1 cup boiling water

Place the daylily buds and tree ear mushrooms in separate bowls and soak each with ½ cup of boiling water for 30 minutes. Drain the daylily buds and cut off the stem ends. Drain the tree ears and cut off any woody spots. Rinse briefly, squeeze dry, and set aside.

Sauce

2 Tbs. tamari soy sauce
1 Tbs. (heaping) Hoisin sauce
1 Tbs. rice wine or sherry
2 Tbs. vegetable stock or water
½-1 tsp. hot chili paste (optional)

Mix together sauce ingredients and set aside.

3 Tbs. peanut oil
1 Tbs. fresh ginger root, grated and peeled
3 garlic cloves, minced or pressed
1 medium onion
½ small cabbage, shredded
2 bell peppers (1 red and 1 green), thinly sliced
2 medium carrots, grated
2 cups bean sprouts
8 oz. tofu, cubed (combined with 1 tsp. five spice powder)
6 scallions, thinly sliced
12 Mandarin Pancakes (see the following recipe)
1 cup Hoisin sauce

Heat a wok on medium-high heat for 30 seconds. Add the peanut oil and heat for 30 seconds before adding the ginger and garlic. Stir-fry for 1 minute. Add the onion and cabbage and stir-fry for 2 minutes, lowering the heat a bit if the vegetables stick or begin to brown. Add the peppers and stir-fry for 1 minute before adding the carrots and bean sprouts. Stir-fry for 30 seconds. Finally, add the daylily buds, tree ear mushrooms, Five-spice Tofu, and the sauce to the sauté. Stir-fry until heated through (about 3 minutes.)

Transfer the Mu Shu Vegetables to a platter, top with sliced scallions, and serve with warm Mandarin Pancakes and Hoisin sauce. Spread each pancake with about a teaspoon of Hoisin sauce and a couple of heaping tablespoons of Mu Shu Vegetables. Roll the pancake up. While this can be eaten with your hands, knives and forks are recommended for the fastidious.

(Moosewood Collective 1990)

Hot and Sour Soup

¼ lb. boneless pork or 2 pork chops (½-inch thick), trimmed, boned and cut into ⅛-inch square strips, about 2 inches long, equal to ½ cup of strips.

2 tsp. cornstarch

Shredding is easier if the pork is partially frozen. Sprinkle cornstarch over pork shreds, using fingers to coat evenly.

6 dried tree ear mushrooms (1 scant Tbs. broken pieces)
4 dried daylily buds
2 large dried black mushrooms (2-inch size)
3 oz. bamboo shoots, drained
1 cake (3" x 3" x ¾") fresh bean curd
2 scallions

Soak tree ear mushrooms and daylily buds separately in warm water for at least 20 minutes each or until softened.

Rinse tree ears well; cut off any hard parts, and then cut each in 2 or 3 pieces. Pinch off hard ends of daylily buds and cut in half. Cover dried black mushrooms with ½ cup warm water and let stand at least 20 minutes, then squeeze the soaking liquid out and save it. Trim and discard mushroom stems, and slice the mushrooms into narrow strips. Set dried ingredients aside on a plate. Shred bamboo shoots into 2- by ⅛-inch strips, and add to the plate of dried ingredients.

Rinse the bean curd cake and split it in half horizontally to make 2 thin cakes. Then cut it into ¼-inch strips, 1 ½ inches long.

Chop scallions fine; set aside for garnish.

Egg petals

    1 egg

Beat egg in a liquid measuring cup (with lip) just long enough to blend yolk with white.

Soup base

    3½ cups chicken broth (fresh or canned)
    1 Tbs. dark soy sauce
    1 Tbs. rice wine or dry sherry
    ½ tsp. salt
    ½ tsp. black pepper (or to taste)

Combine ingredients with reserved mushroom liquid in a 3-quart saucepan.

    2 Tbs. rice vinegar or red wine vinegar
    2 Tbs. cornstarch dissolved in 2 Tbs. water
    1 Tbs. sesame oil

Have vinegar, dissolved cornstarch, and sesame oil at hand; do not combine. Red wine vinegar is sharper than

Chinese vinegar; you may want to use slightly less than 2 Tbs.

Bring the soup base to a boil. Add the pork strips; stir to separate. Then add the tree ears, daylily buds, black mushrooms, and bamboo shoots. Simmer and cook gently 2 to 3 minutes, or until pork is cooked through.

Add the bean curd and bring slowly to a boil. Stir the cornstarch mixture, then add to the soup and stir gently until the soup thickens and is clear. Simmer while stirring in the vinegar.

Stir until the soup swirls in the pan. Slowly add the beaten egg (in a thin stream) into the soup, pouring at the edge of the pan. As soon as all the egg is added, remove from heat. Let stand until the egg forms petals which float to the surface (almost instantly). The egg petals will be thin and delicate if directions are accurately followed. Boiling the soup will disburse them; overcooking will harden them.

Ladle into 6 individual soup bowls. Garnish each bowl with a little of the chopped scallions and float ½ tsp. sesame oil on each. If serving from a soup tureen, garnish it with the entire amount of scallions and oil. Makes 6 servings.

(Myers 1984)

And, finally, if you are looking for something *really* unique, Dees Adam-Melb (1969) offers the following recipe for

Sajur Kimblo (Indonesian Vegetables):

½ cup cloud tree ear mushrooms
½ cup transparent noodles
½ cup dried daylily buds
1 medium onion, chopped
1 clove garlic, crushed
2 Tbs. butter
3 cups chicken broth
lemon juice to taste
ketjap (Indonesian soy sauce)
¼ tsp. ginger
salt and pepper to taste
1 cup string beans, sliced
1 cup celery, sliced
1 cup leeks, thinly sliced
1 cup bean sprouts
onion flakes for garnish

Soak mushrooms, transparent noodles, and dried daylily buds in water for 10 minutes. Drain and cut lily buds into ½ inch pieces, discarding any hard pieces.

Sauté onion and garlic in butter until transparent, but not brown. Season chicken broth with lemon juice and ketjap. Add broth to kettle with ginger. Salt and pepper to taste. Bring to a boil. Add sliced string beans and celery. Simmer 5 minutes. Add leeks (cleaned and thinly sliced), bean sprouts, cloud ears, noodles, and lily buds. Garnish with onion flakes and serve.

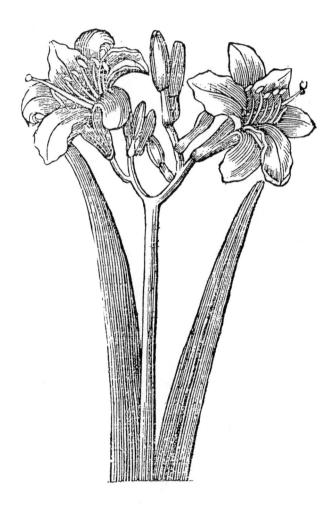

One must admit that this interesting and beautiful roadside flower is also a wild food plant of no mean order, and is even worthy of a place in our vegetable gardens.

Euell Gibbons, *Stalking the Wild Asparagus*

Chapter 5

Recipes for Blossoms

Today, cooking with flowers has become very trendy. Nasturtiums are used in salads; squash flowers are made into fritters, and chrysanthemums are used in salads and as tea. We often forget that flowers and flower buds have a long culinary history in the western world — broccoli and cauliflower are both clusters of flower buds!

Daylily flowers stay open only one day and then wither, but there are so many of them and so many waiting in their buds for a chance on stage that it appears as if they are always in flower. Their beauty and flavor have stimulated the imagination of many cooks.

Daylily buds and flowers may be harvested any time during the blooming stage. Daylilies of almost any color can be used, but the yellow, orange, pale pinks and pastels seem to have the best flavor. Red flowers are often bitter. Always remove anthers and stamens from the flowers before using them.

Since flavor is often a reflection of fragrance (those which smell sweet also end up tasting sweet), flavor depends on the aromatic characteristics of the variety you choose. This also makes a bit of experimenting necessary, because the flavor of certain varieties may not be compatible with other ingredients in these recipes.

According to Bill Owen of Ohio State University Extension, Lake County, daylily flowers should be collected, washed, and placed on newspaper to dry. When using, soak them in water and then add them to recipes.

Recipes using daylily flowers span the range from appetizers and soup to dessert and include a couple of breads and biscuits! In China and Japan, the flowers are dried and stored for use as a thickener for soups, and the petals add a delicate flavor to clear soups. Fresh, withered, or dried flowers are added to soups in the last few minutes of cooking. The most basic way of preparing daylily flowers is as a vegetable side dish.

According to Cathy Wilkinson Barash, frozen daylily flowers are just as good as fresh, and make a neat mid-winter treat. To freeze, blanch either the flowers or buds for 3 minutes in boiling water, then plunge them immediately into ice water. After they are cooled, pat them dry and pack them in freezer bags.

One of the best known uses of daylily flowers is in the form of fritters, which can be served as a snack, an hors d'oeuvre, a vegetable side dish, or, sprinkled with powdered sugar or dipped in jam or sour cream, as a dessert. Barash also suggests adding their delightful flavor to blueberry pancakes.

Sautéed Daylilies

12 daylily flowers
2 chive flowers broken into florets
½ tsp salt

Put all ingredients into a frying pan or wok. Cover and simmer just until all the moisture is cooked away and the flowers are tender. Don't overcook. Serve hot. Butter or margarine may be added for flavor.

(Barash 1993)

Buttered Daylilies

8 daylily blossoms
1 cup chicken broth
3 Tbs. butter
    salt and pepper to taste

Simmer the daylilies for 4-5 minutes in the chicken broth. Drain, add butter, salt, and pepper to taste, and serve. Makes four servings.

Daylily Fritters

    1 egg
    1 cup milk
    1 cup flour
    ½ tsp. salt
    ⅛ tsp. pepper
    2 cups cooking oil
    3 dozen fresh daylily flowers (or buds)

Mix egg, milk, flour, salt, and pepper in a medium bowl to make a thick batter. Heat the oil in a saucepan to about 375°F. Dip each flower in the batter, drop into oil, and fry to a golden brown. Do several at a time. Remove with a slotted spoon and drain on a paper towel.

Sprinkle with salt (as hors d'oeuvre or vegetable dish) or provide powdered sugar, jam or sour cream at the table for dipping. You might also try these with Blue Strawbery dipping sauce (see recipe on page 30).

Daylily buds and blossoms have almost as much protein as spinach, more vitamin A than string beans, and about the same amount of vitamin C as orange juice.

Daylily Blueberry Pancakes

4 eggs
1 cup cottage cheese
⅛ tsp. salt
2 Tbs. oil
½ cup sifted all-purpose flour
1 Tbs. granulated sugar
½ tsp. vanilla
  petals from 10 daylilies, coarsely chopped
1 cup blueberries

Mix the first seven ingredients in a blender or food processor, and blend until smooth. Pour into a bowl. Gently stir in daylily petals and blueberries. Let sit 10 minutes. Drop by the ¼ cupful onto a hot, lightly greased griddle or skillet over medium heat. Cook until bubbles on top of pancakes break, then turn over and brown the other side. They may be served plain, with the syrup of your choice, or with butter and syrup. Serves 4.

(Barash 1993)

Daylily flowers can be a highlight in any part of your meal — from soup through dessert. Here's how. First, there is a simple, clear soup:

Basic Daylily Flower Soup

    4 cups chicken stock
    1 cup daylily flowers, cut into 1" pieces
    ¼ cup onions, cut into very thin rings
    1 Tbs. mushrooms, diced

Bring chicken stock to a boil and add other ingredients. Simmer for 5 minutes. Serves 4. Soy sauce can be added for extra seasoning.

(Rombauer and Becker 1953)

I would expect a book such as The Chinese Restaurant Cookbook *or* Madame Wu's Art of Chinese Cooking *to have daylily recipes, having learned, while researching my own book that Chinese hot and sour soup is somwhat like Jewish chicken soup -- every cook has a variation. What surprised me was that* The Joy of Cooking *has daylily recipes.*
Cathy Wilkinson Barash

Or you might wish a more complicated one:

Daylily Chicken Soup

5 cups chicken stock
½ cup chicken, boiled and minced
1½ inch cube of salt pork
¾ cup potatoes, boiled and diced
2 Tbs. onion, minced
3 Tbs. celery, minced
¼ tsp. ginger
   salt and pepper to taste
2 Tbs. flour
2 Tbs. sherry
3 Tbs. mushrooms, minced
1½ cups daylily blossoms, chopped
1 Tbs. parsley
1 Tbs. soy sauce

Combine chicken stock, chicken, salt pork, potatoes, onion, celery, ginger, salt, and pepper and cook 10-15 minutes on medium high heat. Remove salt pork. Turn down heat to simmer. Add flour dissolved in sherry, the mushrooms, parsley, soy sauce, and daylilies, and simmer 3-4 minutes. Serve.

(Smith 1973)

Now for salad. Here are four choices, ranging from simple to complex:

Summertime Salad

½ large cucumber, thinly sliced
2 tomatoes
1 head lettuce, chopped
6 yellow and orange daylilies, chopped
½ red onion, thinly sliced

Combine thinly sliced cucumbers, fresh tomato wedges, chopped lettuce, chopped yellow or orange daylilies, and thin red onion rings. Chill salad and toss with dressing of your choice before serving.

Daylily Chicken Salad Special

1½ cups chicken, boiled and diced
½ cup celery, finely chopped
¼ cup chutney
1 Tbs. capers
1 Tbs. candied ginger, minced
   Salt and pepper
2 daylily blossoms
2 small lettuce leaves

Combine all ingredients except blossoms and lettuce, and toss with the following dressing:

¼ cup each lemon juice, mayonnaise, and honey
½ tsp. dried tarragon

To assemble on individual salad plates, place some lettuce, then spread open daylily flowers on each plate and fill with the chicken salad. Serves 2.

(Smith 1973)

Aspic-Filled Daylily Blossoms

10 washed daylily blossoms, anthers and stamens
   removed
1 pkg. (3 oz.) lemon gelatin
1 cup boiling water
1 can (16 oz.) stewed tomatoes, cut up
1 tsp. lemon juice
1 tsp. white wine
  Worcestershire sauce
1 heaping tsp. horseradish
1-2 dashes hot pepper sauce
½ tsp. dried basil
¼ tsp. dill weed
½ tsp. minced onion
1 can (8 ½ oz.) artichoke hearts, drained and quar-
   tered

Dissolve gelatin in boiling water. Stir in tomatoes, lemon
juice, white wine, Worcestershire sauce, horseradish, hot
pepper sauce, basil, dill, onion, and artichoke hearts. Cool
to room temperature. Place blossoms in wine glasses to
keep them upright. Fill blossoms with aspic. Chill in
refrigerator until aspic is firm. Place filled blossoms on
lettuce leaves and garnish center with sour cream, dust with
paprika and decorate flower base with fresh opal basil
leaves.

(Jay Szabo of Sunnybrook Farms,
quoted in Beal 1988)

Daylily Asparagus Salad

1 dozen asparagus tips, about 4 inches long
2 chopped daylilies blossoms
  chicory, dandelion greens, spinach or leaf lettuce
4 Tbs. salad oil
1 Tbs. wine vinegar
1 tsp. lemon juice
1 Tbs. honey
  pinch dry mustard
¼ tsp. salt
  several grinds of fresh pepper
1 Tbs. capers

Cook the asparagus until barely tender (about 7 minutes), then plunge into ice water. Drain. Prepare the daylilies and cut into ¾" lengths. Place the chilled asparagus on a bed of greens and sprinkle the daylilies over it. Prepare a dressing with the oil, vinegar, lemon, honey, dry mustard, salt, and pepper. Shake well and pour the mixture over the salad. Sprinkle on the capers and serve. Serves 4.

(Smith 1973)

Because daylilies have long been a significant part of Asian cuisine, you can buy an eight ounce bag of dried daylily buds for less than a dollar in any Asian grocery store in the U.S. under the names "dried lily buds," "golden needles" or "gum jum." Or, you can harvest these same flower buds for free in your garden.

Next, your choice of five entrees:

Chicken Daylily Commotion

4 Tbs. butter
2 boneless chicken breasts
1 cup mushrooms, sliced
2-3 cups daylily blossoms
½ cup onion, chopped
½ cup snow peas, cut diagonally into 1-2" pieces
1½ Tbs. cornstarch
¼ cup chicken broth
2 Tbs. soy sauce
½ tsp. ginger, powder or grated fresh
2 Tbs. dry sherry
1 Tbs. honey
salt and pepper

In a large skillet, melt butter, add sliced chicken and cook 3-4 minutes, stirring to prevent sticking. Add mushrooms, daylilies, onion, snow peas, cornstarch dissolved in broth, soy sauce, ginger, sherry, honey, salt, and pepper to taste.

Continually stir-fry the ingredients in the skillet for 3-4 minutes or until they are fork tender, but not limp. Serve immediately. This is particularly good over rice.

(Smith 1973)

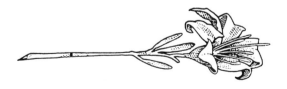

Pork with Daylilies

3 shoulder pork chops, trimmed and cut into small
  pieces
1 tsp. salt
¼ tsp. granulated sugar
1 clove garlic, crushed
1 onion, chopped
1 Tbs. tamari
1 tsp. fresh ginger, chopped
1 Tbs. cornstarch
3 Tbs. peanut oil
1 onion, sliced
1 Tbs. sherry
3 cups daylily flowers
¼ cup water

Mix the meat, salt, sugar, garlic, chopped onion, tamari,
ginger and cornstarch together in a bowl. Allow to sit for
5 minutes. In a large frying pan, heat oil over a medium-
high heat. Add onion slices and sauté until browned. Add
meat mixture and sherry and cook for 3 to 4 minutes,
stirring frequently. Add daylilies, cooked onion and water.
Cook an additional 3 to 4 minutes, and serve immediately.
Serves 4.

(Barash 1993)

---

*Since the time of the Sung Dynasty, (about 1059
A.D.) daylilies (especially the tubers) have been
recognized for their diuretic properties. They may
also act as a laxative, so it is best to eat them in
moderation.*

Cathy Wilkinson Barash
Edible Flowers: From Garden to Palate

Daylily Sausage Tarts

    4 tart shells
    ½ lb. bulk sausage
    ½ lb. mushrooms, sliced
    1 Tbs. minced onions
    1 cup daylilies, chopped
    ¼ cup and 1½ Tbs. butter
    1 Tbs. Madeira wine
    1 Tbs. chopped chives or green onions
    1 Tbs. chopped parsley
    ½ Tbs. lemon juice
        salt and pepper
    1½ Tbs. butter
    1½ Tbs. flour
    1 cup light cream
        additional chives for garnish

Prepare and bake tart shells, using any standard recipe. Cook sausage. Place mushrooms, onion, and daylilies in skillet in which ¼ cup butter has been melted. Sauté 2-3 minutes. Remove from heat, add drained sausage, wine, chives, parsley, lemon, juice, salt and pepper, and stir to blend well.

Prepare a *roux* of 1½ Tbs. butter and the flour, and slowly add cream. Stir until thickened. Add mixture from skillet, blend well and adjust seasonings.

Fill pastry shells, sprinkle with chives and place in oven for 5-10 minutes so they are hot for serving. Makes 4 servings.

(Smith 1973)

If your tastes go to seafood, Barash suggests cooking daylilies with shrimp:

Stir-Fry Daylily Shrimp

> peanut oil
> 1 Tbs. freshly grated ginger
> 1 clove garlic, finely minced
> ½ cup onion, chopped
> 4 daylily buds
> petals from 4 daylily flowers
> 8 oz. mushrooms, sliced
> 1 cup Chinese cabbage, coarsely chopped
> ½ cup red bell pepper, chopped
> 1 lb. medium shrimp, cleaned

Sauce

> 1 tsp. sesame oil
> 1 Tbs. tamari
> 1 tsp. granulated sugar
> 1 Tbs. rice wine vinegar
> 2 Tbs. cornstarch dissolved in 2 Tbs. water

Heat a wok over high heat. When the wok is hot, coat lightly with peanut oil. Add ginger and garlic, stirring constantly. Add onion and cook for 1 minute. Add daylily buds and petals, mushrooms, cabbage and pepper a bit at a time so wok stays hot. Cook for 1 minute, stirring frequently. Add shrimp and cook until they just turn pink.

Mix sauce ingredients together in a bowl. Pour into wok, stirring until sauce turns transparent and glossy, and serve immediately. Serves 4

(Barash 1993)

And, finally, for that special occasion which simply demands duck:

Daylilied Duck

1   duck, cut into serving portions
1   whole onion, studded with several cloves
1   bay leaf
1   tsp. salt
4   Tbs. butter
2   Tbs. cornstarch
2   Tbs. soy sauce
3   Tbs. peanut butter
½   tsp. nutmeg
½   tsp. ginger, powdered or grated fresh
1   Tbs. orange rind, grated
    salt and pepper
1   cup sliced mushrooms
2   cups daylily blossoms, whole or chopped

Place duck, clove-studded onion, bay leaf, and salt in a saucepan with enough water to cover the duck. Cover and simmer for 45 minutes. Drain and dry duck. Strain broth and reserve 2½ cups. Sauté duck in butter until golden brown. Combine cornstarch and soy sauce and add to broth. Stir over medium heat until smooth and thickened. Then add peanut butter, nutmeg, ginger, orange rind, and salt and pepper to taste.

Continue stirring. When broth starts simmering, add mushrooms and daylilies and cook for 3-4 minutes. Pour over duck on a heated serving platter and serve.

(Smith 1973)

Of course, no meal is complete without bread or biscuits, and here again, daylily flowers can provide delicious intrigue! The following two recipes appear in Rombauer and Becker's 1953 edition of *Joy of Cooking*:

Daylily Flower Bread

    3 cups boiling water
    1 cup dried daylily flowers, chopped
    2 packages dried yeast
    ½ cup honey
    3 Tbs. oil
    2 Tbs. dried dulce (red algae) or 1 tsp. salt
    1 cup granola
    1 cup dates, chopped
  5-6 cups unbleached flour

Pour 3 cups of boiling water over 1 cup chopped, dried daylily flowers. Let stand until water has cooled to luke-warm. Add yeast, honey, oil, dulce or salt, granola, and dates. Stir until mixed. Gradually add 5-6 cups unbleached flour. Mix the flour first with a spoon and then with your hands. When the dough leaves the sides of the bowl, stop adding flour. Punch down. Divide dough into 2 pieces. Knead each piece, adding flour as necessary until dough is smooth and elastic. Shape into a ball and place in a greased bowl, turning to grease top of dough. Cover. Let rise until double in bulk. Knead. Shape into two loaves. Let rise again until almost double in bulk. Bake at 400° for 30-36 minutes.

Confetti Biscuits

2   each, orange and yellow daylily flowers
4   sprigs parsley
4   heads red bee balm flowers, petals only
¾   cup milk
¼   cup wheat germ
1¾ cups unbleached flour
2½ tsp. baking powder
½   tsp. baking soda
¼   cup shortening

Cut daylily flowers and parsley into small pieces. Add bee balm petals, and combine with milk.

In a bowl, mix flour, wheat germ, baking powder and baking soda. Cut in shortening until dough is like coarse crumbs, and then combine with the first mixture. Shape into a ball. Knead on a floured surface. Flatten and cut into biscuits. Bake at 450°F for 12-15 minutes.

For dessert, try light, puffy Daylily Fritters (see the recipe on page 48).

You've now made an elegant, full-course meal with daylily flowers in every dish. How's that for versatility?

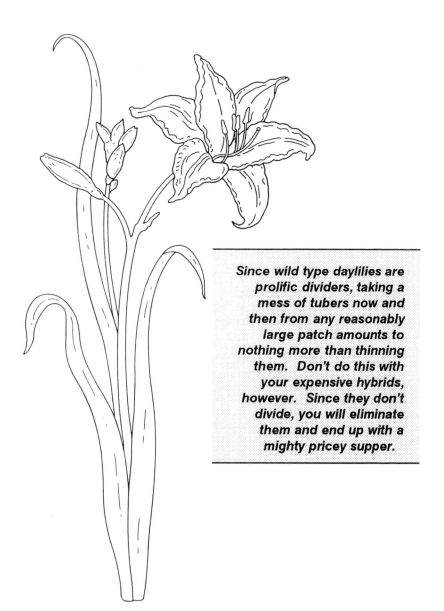

Since wild type daylilies are prolific dividers, taking a mess of tubers now and then from any reasonably large patch amounts to nothing more than thinning them. Don't do this with your expensive hybrids, however. Since they don't divide, you will eliminate them and end up with a mighty pricey supper.

Chapter 6

Recipes for Daylily Pods

T he three-angled, three-loculed daylily pods, while young, small and fleshy, are also valuable food. To put "young" in perspective, the daylily pod, or fruit, matures over about a 60-day period from fertilization to actual release of seed, during which it progresses from a green fleshy pod to a dry brown one. Therefore a three to six-day-old pod is still pretty close to the flower!

The following two recipes from Rombauer and Becker's *Joy of Cooking* are specifically for the young pods. Pods can also be used in many of the recipes calling for buds.

Daylily Pods as a Vegetable

2 cups daylily pods
  butter
  salt
  pepper

Wash 3 and 4-day-old pods thoroughly and slice them crosswise, but do not remove the seeds. These pods make attractive green trefoils. Add 1 and 2-day-old pods whole. Boil, steam, or sauté them for about 10 minutes, add butter, salt and pepper, and serve as a side dish.

Daylily Pod Pickles

2 cups daylily pods, 3-5 days old
2 Tbs. salt, non-iodized
1 cup water
1¼ vinegar
1 cup sugar

Prepare a clean, hot, sterilized pint jar.   Gather and wash 2 cups of 3 to 5-day-old pods. Dissolve 2 Tbs. non-iodized salt in 1 cup of water. Soak the fruits in this mixture for 24 hours. Drain and pack them in the jar.

Boil 1¼ cups vinegar and 1 cup sugar for 2 minutes. Pour this mixture over the pods. Seal the jar and refrigerate. Let pickles marinate four weeks before eating.

Chapter 7

The Beginnings and Thanks

T he information and recipes included here just scratch the surface of daylily lore. Many more recipes exist in many more cookbooks and many more kitchens. We are constantly searching for recipes and interesting stories about wild growing, volunteer vegetables and fruits. If you have some to share, please write to Goosefoot Acres Press, at the address on the back cover. Space permitting, we will include your contributions in the next revision of the appropriate book or booklet and will attribute them to you. We thank the following for the recipes included here:

Adam-Melb, Dees. 1969. "Rijsttafel," *Gourmet Magazine* 29(8):14, 49.

Apps, Darrel. 1995. Personal communication, Woodside Gardens, Bridgeton, NJ.

Baracz, Jan. 1981. Personal communication, Chardon, OH.

Barash, Cathy Wilkinson. 1993. *Edible Flowers: From Garden to Palate.* Fulcrum Publishing, Golden, CO. pp.25-31

Beal, Eileen. 1988. "The Fine Art of Cooking with Flowers," *Western Reserve Magazine*. June, 1988 pp. 43-51.

Crowhurst, Adrienne. n.d. *The Weed Cookbook*. Lancer Books, New York, NY.

Crowhurst, Adrienne. n.d. *The Flower Cookbook*. Lancer Books, New York, NY.

Duke, James A. 1992. *Handbook of Edible Weeds*. CRC Press, Boca Raton, FL

Facciola, S. 1990. *Cornucopia — A Source Book of Edible Plants*. Kampong Publication, Vista, CA.

Foster, Steven and Yue Chongxi. 1991. Daylilies — Xuancao. *Herbal Emissaries — Bringing Chinese Herbs to the West*. Healing Arts Press, Rochester, VT.

Haller, James. 1976. *The Blue Strawbery Cookbook*. Harvard Common Press, Cambridge, MA.

Kluger, Marilyn. 1984. *The Wild Flavor*. Jeremy P. Tarcher, Los Angeles, CA.

Moosewood Collective. 1990. *Sundays at Moosewood Restaurant*. Simon & Schuster/Fireside, New York. NY.

Myers, Barbara. 1984. *The Chinese Restaurant Cookbook*. Greenwich House.

Owen, Bill. 1978. *Newsletter*. The Ohio State University, Lake County Extension, Painesville, OH.

Rombauer, Irma S. and Marion R. Becker. 1953. *Joy of Cooking*. Bobbs-Merrill Company, Inc. NY.

Russell, Helen Ross. 1975. *Foraging for Dinner — Collecting and Cooking Wild Foods*. Thomas Nelson, Inc., Nashville, TN.

Smith, Leona Woodring. 1973. *The Forgotten Art of Flower Cookery*. Harper and Row, NY.

Tatum, Billy Joe. 1976. *Billy Joe Tatum's Wild Foods Cookbook*. Workman Press.

Wu, Madame. 1973. *Madame Wu's Art of Chinese Cooking*. Bantam Press.

Index

AVAILABLE FROM GOOSEFOOT ACRES

Plain & Happy Living — Amish Recipes and Remedies Autobiography and folk medicine handbook of an Old Order Amish woman widowed at age 33 with 10 children. Herbal remedies, recipes for household products and delicious foods on a very low budget, interwoven with wonderfully warm stories and anecdotes. **By Emma Byler, 160 pages, 21 illus., 6 x 9 paperback (ISBN 1-879863-71-5)** **$9.95**

Living Simply — Lessons from the Amish Lifestyle The Amish have much to teach us about practical economics, raising children and low overhead, self-sufficient living. This book introduces their culture and focuses on how the Amish raise children which can be adapted to non-Amish society. **By Peter A. Gail, Ph.D., approx. 160 pages, 5 ½ x 8 ½ paperback, illustr. (Available Spring 1996)** **$10.95**

The Dandelion Celebration — A Guide to Unexpected Cuisine What's the best thing to do about your dandelions? EAT THEM! Discover the history and nutritional and medicinal properties of this lawnscaping arch villain as you learn how to pick, prepare, and savor every part of the plant! **By Peter A. Gail, Ph.D., 160 pages, 9 photos, 5 ½ x 8 ½ paperback (ISBN 1-879863-51-0)** **$10.95**

The Totally Free Lunch — Harvesting Your Backyard Growing and wild-crafting weeds for food is a multi-million a year industry! Stop wasting good vegetables. Recipes for and facts about over 20 common backyard weeds, plus a curriculum unit which introduces children to the culinary marvels of the dandelion. **By Peter A. Gail, Ph.D., 250 pages, paperback, with illustrations. (Available Spring 1996)** **$15.95**

The Delightful Delicious Daylily — Recipes and More, 2nd Edition. Recipes for "tubers," shoots, buds, flowers, and fruits of the daylily, plus plant history and cultivation. Includes sources of further information on the daylily for serious enthusiasts. **By Peter A. Gail, Ph.D., 70 pages, 5 ½ x 8 ½ paperback (ISBN 1-879863-60-X).** **$6.95**

Violets in Your Kitchen. Violet flowers and greens are not only tasty, but are nature's second richest source of Vitamin C. These 35 recipes for appetizers, salads, soups, ice creams and other desserts will help you capitalize on all this goodness. **By Peter A. Gail, Ph.D. 58 pages, paperback.** **$5.95**

Dandy-Blend Instant Dandelion Beverage Delicious instant roasted beverage made from extracts of roasted dandelion root, barley and rye. Tastes similar to coffee but without caffeine. Naturally sweetened with its own fructose. **3 oz. (85 gm.) container makes about 70 cups (6 - 8 cents a cup!)** Imported from Canada. Write for separate brochure. **$5.95**

ORDER FORM

Name: _____

Address: _____

City/State: _____ Zip _____

Telephone: (___) _____ Date: _____

QUAN-TITY	TITLE/ PRODUCT DESCRIPTION	COST PER ITEM*	TOTAL

*Prices subject to change without notice. Please enclose check or money order with order slip. Make checks payable to GOOSEFOOT ACRES, INC. DO NOT SEND CASH. Ohio residents add 7% sales tax. SHIPPING: Please add $3.50 for the first item ordered and $1.00 for each additional item.	SUB-TOTAL:
	SALES TAX:
Please bill my VISA/MASTERCARD: Acct. No. _____	SHIP-PING:
Expiration Date _____ Signature _____	TOTAL DUE:

SHIP TO: (If different than above)

Name: _____

Address: _____

City/State: _____ Zip _____

MAIL THIS ORDER FORM AND PAYMENT TO:
Goosefoot Acres, Inc.,
P. O. Box 18016, Cleveland, Ohio 44118
QUESTIONS? Call (216) 932-2145
CREDIT CARD ORDERS BY PHONE: (800) 697-4858